Daily Devotions
from the Heart

TAMARA WEAVER

NEWMAN SPRINGS PUBLISHING
320 Broad Street
Red Bank, NJ 07701

First originally published by Newman
Springs Publishing 2024

ISBN 979-8-89061-046-1 (Paperback)
ISBN 979-8-89061-047-8 (Digital)

Printed in the United States of America

Dedicated to God Almighty

Day 1

Trusting Our Savior

There are several factors to examine when learning to trust our Savior. Did we feel safe while trusting our earthly fathers? What kind of role model did they demonstrate? Trusting the wrong person can be a problem when our answer to these questions is a blatant NO! Our Heavenly Father always sets a positive role model for his children. Many folks do not understand the awesome gift of unconditional love.

I always felt as if there were conditions placed upon me to be loved. We have to consider where our earthly fathers were coming from. Did they trust their fathers, or did their early father set a good role model for them? Once more, our humanness comes into play when taking a long, hard look inside the hearts of our earthly fathers. Did some type of abuse take place? Were we violated in some manner? Did we experience feeling safe in our homes? It is imperative to closely examine these factors.

Knowing God as Father is an experience none of us knows how to handle when we first surrender our hearts and lives to Christ, especially if a trust issue exists. As we journey down this road, we will learn by trial and error to trust our Heavenly Father. As humans, we want to analyze our circumstances and try to figure out the happenings of our daily lives. Leaning not on our own understanding but truly placing our faith and trust in our Heavenly Father doesn't happen immediately.

As for me, I am so hardheaded that it took some very painful lessons and many trips around the same mountain before I finally surrendered everything to Christ. I refer to my early Christian walk as being in boot camp—preparing for the battles and sharpening my artillery; putting on the shield of faith, shoes of peace, and loin cloth; learning through repeatedly going in and out of battles; and then taking time to do an inventory of what works and what doesn't. We need to use the weapons provided for us through Christ as his soldiers because we really are in a major battle. Our weapons are not carnal but of a spiritual nature. Taking authority over the darts shot at us by the enemy and his army of darkness and negativity has been a test of my faith in His words of strength and power.

The enemy must believe and will tremble at the mention of the sweet name of Jesus. The power placed in our care came from the blood that flowed from Calvary as Christ died for our salvation. Then why do many of us still remain in bondage if the price has already been paid? Our battles are not carnal but are sent to us from the prince of the air, and our weapons are of a spiritual nature.

> *Trust in the LORD with all your heart and lean not on your own understanding; in all your ways acknowledge Him, and He shall direct your paths. (Proverbs 3:5–6)*

Lord, thank you for giving us the spiritual weapons necessary to claim total victory over the prince of the air.

Guarding Our Minds

It is important what we allow to enter our minds. Feeding our souls with things of this world will not give us the strength we need to successfully conquer our enemies! Pleading the blood over our minds, our dwellings, our children, and our families is essential, as is bidding the protection of our angels, who are waiting for us to call on them to enter our realm and fight our battles for us.

God gives us celestial beings to walk with us and ward off the darts of our enemy. Our angels are wise and strong and can take a fiery dart and crush it as if it were only a tiny toothpick. Do we fully comprehend just how much power we have in the name of Jesus Christ? Grasping this concept will only assist us in our ongoing battles.

As parents and grandparents, it is most definitely our place to protect the young minds of our offspring and family members who are rendered helpless when it comes to fighting spiritual battles. We must stand in the gap for those who do not know how to fight effectively. They are clueless when it comes to practicing productive strategies when in a spiritual battle. Many worship the Lord but don't seem to utilize the power we have in Jesus' name. The closer we seek after Christ, the more the enemy comes against us with his best fleet of demons. He has trained them to provoke us or push our buttons as an irritant if we do not possess the knowledge to avoid his attacks.

Truthfully, most of our biggest battles are fought in our minds. It can be a difficult task to replace the information gathered in our minds. We need to cast wrong information out and replace it with thoughts of goodness and love. Have you ever done something out of the ordinary compared to what has been established as your normal behavior? Then take the time to ask yourself, Where did that come from? Even our talk can be a hindrance when we have been conditioned to talk in a certain manner. How do we change the words that flow out of our mouths at times?

I began to look closely at the life of Christ. He had no hidden agendas or ulterior motives, saying what he meant and meaning what he said. Why is it so difficult for us to speak cautiously?

> *You will keep him in perfect peace, whose mind is stayed on you, because he trusts in you. (Isaiah 26:3)*

A man speaks what is hidden in his heart. Learning to cast down vain imaginations that come against our minds helps us replace these thoughts with words of loveliness and strength, training ourselves to speak godly.

Thank you, Lord, for providing us the tools to guard our minds.

Speaking the Truth

Have you ever thought about a time when someone spoke a word of truth to you when you weren't expecting it? Did it upset you or perhaps cause your flesh to rise to say, "Now wait just a minute"? Maybe when those words were spoken, you did not get it. Then later, when you had grown spiritually while gaining maturity, you realized the words spoken that once offended you were the truth. Well, we probably needed to hear it anyway, but it may have taken some time for these words to register in our spirit. At times, our hearts are not ready to hear the truth, but God knew we needed to hear it. He knew that, in time, it would finally register with us.

I personally have heard sermons over and over again, and then out of the blue, it hits home! Maybe our ears and hearts were not prepared to hear the truth. However, it did us much good. I am amazed at how God allows us to hear things, and when we are ready, we will understand. It has happened to me several times in my life, and when it sank in, it was a divine revelation. I am talking about matters of Christianity—not trivial words like your house needs a good cleaning, but words that strengthen us or propel our spiritual growth! Then suddenly, you get what they were trying to tell you.

Truth hurts, but I would rather have a word of truth spoken to me and have it sting for a short while than a lie that may last an entire lifetime. The truth works to set us free, while a lie keeps us bound up. The spoken word is powerful, and being cautious about speaking nonsense is a good habit to practice. Many people are not walking on the same spiritual level as you. Speaking words that are of a positive nature is always best. "So speaketh a man from his heart," and when our hearts are burdened and fearful, it takes much energy and effort on our part not to speak negatively about our circumstances.

We attract whatever words come out of our mouths. It is a tedious task to rise above our situations and to speak words of faith and hope. Over the years, I have tried to train myself to speak words that benefit me and those who may be in hearing distance. Maybe if things are not changing or improving in your life, consider what type of words you are speaking. The power of the spoken word brings power to your daily life. Practice speaking words that bring hope and peace to an otherwise negative situation.

> *Then Jesus said to those Jews who believed Him, "If you abide in My word, you are My disciples indeed. And you shall know the truth and the truth shall make you free." (John 8:31–32)*

Just like when the God of our soul told the earth to bring forth light on day number one when creating our world, there was light! Let us begin to speak words of strength and delight to the ears of our Heavenly Father. Let us praise Him both in word and deed.

Thank you, Lord, for always speaking the truth, for the truth will set you free.

Renewing Our Minds

Let's explore what it truly means to "be ye transformed by the renewing of your mind," as stated in the Word of God. Well, how do we renew our minds? First, we start by filling our minds and our spirits with the Word of God, as well as being aware of the idea that the enemy wants us to get stuck in our past and remind us of our many mistakes or having some very hurtful regrets. You take your mind captive and tell the enemy you are not going there today, or any other day for that matter!

Purposely dwell on things that are lovely and positive. Maybe you would call me simple when it comes to keeping these thoughts from engulfing me daily. I enjoy watching something light and funny on TV or listening to comforting and soothing music.

Occasionally, I will watch a sitcom, listen to children's music, or just spend time with my grandchildren and play silly games just to make them laugh. When we stop to think about our past, we will find there are far more pleasant memories than unhappy ones. It takes ten positives to negate one negative.

Recently, I began thinking of all the people who have blessed me over the years. I have received more blessings than other unfruitful words spoken against me, words that were meant to harm me. I remembered just how many folks have blessed me financially, or loans I was supposed to pay back but never did, and yet my debts were canceled by the hand of God! They weren't large debts, but they emerged from my subconscious, where they had been stored in my memory banks, and as God provided the money, I began the process of paying everyone back. It reminded me how often we forget to give to the storehouse where we gain strength and fellowship with other believers.

I have experienced debt cancellation. Does God refuse to bless us when we don't give Him what is rightfully His? No, of course not; He doesn't withhold from His children. I love to give what is appropriated to me to God and to bless others around me. Knowing what a loving and generous God we serve makes me know I am loved unconditionally.

Giving breaks the bonds our enemy thinks he has placed between us and God. God doesn't need our money, He owns the cattle on a thousand hills, grazing on rich, green grass. If we are selfish and hoard what he has so richly blessed us with, what have we gained? We certainly cannot take it with us when we leave this earth. Being generous is a good thing, and it states that if a man has a need and you have the means to meet that need, whether it be financial or if he only needs a drink of cool water or something to nourish his body, or maybe a place to lay his head at night, and we refuse to meet these needs by looking the other way, we have sinned against God and his commandments.

> *Do not be conformed to this world, but be transformed by the renewing of your mind, that you may prove what is that good and acceptable and perfect will of God. (Romans 12:2)*

Lord, thank you for allowing us to choose to renew our minds daily and to bless others with the resources you have provided us.

Day 5

Gratitude

Today, as I awakened, an overwhelming sense of gratitude filled my heart—remembering when I first became acquainted with my Lord. I had no idea just how much he cares for his children. Growing up in what seemed to me to be a judgmental and critical church, I developed a pattern of thinking that I had to be perfect for Christ to love me. Well, even in my own family, messing up was not an option. Realizing our humanness and knowing that God created us, helped me understand that He knew we would make mistakes from time to time.

I had walked in a fog of guilt, shame, and self-condemnation for so long, all the while desiring to serve God faithfully. For me, reality was just too painful to handle. I tried to live up to the standards people had set for me. Our Christian walk cannot be about people but only about a relationship with Christ. People will let you down, and you can count on that. When I finally began to feel the love Christ has for me, my guilt, shame, and self-condemnation began to fade away, never to return.

Many of us have made serious blunders during our lifetime. Certainly, the only perfect human was Christ. Letting go of such detrimental feelings and replacing them with the joy of the Lord are the reasons I would tell anyone of his desire for his children to be free. It wasn't until I was delivered of codependency that the reality of my blunders began to haunt me. The enemy was relentless with his accusing nature, telling me that "God can never use you because of your sins" and "if people knew what you have done in the past."

I began to resist the enemy very energetically by telling him he is a liar and to get behind me, for I am persevering to have my heart and life restored. I will not allow the enemy to interfere in my restoration ever again. Once I discovered this close and extremely intimate relationship with Christ, the sadness and shame began to grow dim and eventually left forever. When the enemy tries to remind me of my past, I just remind him of his future. I am a victor, not a victim. I am just a human being trying my best to serve my Lord and Savior—a vessel of goodness and love, always ready to tell others about His marvelous gift so freely given. It totally blows me away to finally receive this kind of love and to fully understand that if I had been the only person alive on that dreadful day He was crucified, Jesus would have died just for me. It took time to understand His ongoing and lasting unconditional love. For the first time in a very dry season, I emotionally felt free to experience the joy of the Lord. Today, I can say I have been set free!

Oh, give thanks to the LORD, for He is good! For his mercy endures forever. (Psalm 107:1)

Therefore if the Son makes you free, you shall be free indeed. (John 8:36)

When He was on the cross, I was on His mind. Lord, thank you for everything.

God Is Always Good

My pastor always says that life isn't always fair, but God is always good! You've got that right! Life is often puzzling, and trying to analyze things only makes it even more complicated. I once heard, "What is, just is!" God's blessings will chase you down when and only when you place your trust in Him alone. I am a behaviorist and have spent many wasted hours trying to figure out why some people act like they do. Now that I have gained more wisdom, all I can say is this: Just let it go. Without countless wasted hours trying to understand why they acted as they did, it makes my life less stressful and much more enjoyable. All of us have gone through some very unfair things, but have we ever had to say God wasn't good? If our prayers are not answered the way we thought they should, or if they don't get answered the way we wanted them to, it doesn't mean God doesn't answer our prayers.

In his wisdom and sovereignty, He knows what is best for us. Do we always give our children everything they ask for? Of course, we, as parents, cannot always give them what they want. Also, as parents, we know the outcome of such requests. Would we give our child permission to walk out in front of a semitruck just to cross the highway quicker? Waiting for the highway to clear is the safer way to cross the intersection. God sees the great, big picture and knows that certain requests will be harmful or totally destructive. It seems logical to our human minds.

As our Heavenly Father, He loves us enough to make us wait for the timing of God to manifest itself. It is the same as if your small child would ever ask to ride a ten-speed bicycle! Would we say, "Sure, go ahead, and I will even buy you a bike for you to learn on"? WRONG! We would just laugh and tell them, "You are much too young to do that now. Just wait a few years, and I am sure you can learn to ride a ten-speed bike without training wheels."

We must have the patience to take it one step at a time, taking time to grow spiritually, for much responsibility accompanies many of our requests.

"Well, Lord, I only desire to serve you and to preach to thousands and tell them of your gift of salvation." What could possibly be wrong with my request? There are many different elements to discover when you are launching such a serious and profound request. We must grow in wisdom and maturity when handling spiritual issues. There is much to consider when asking for something as important as having a ministry—learning to lean on His wisdom and learning to trust His timing.

You go through spiritual boot camp, as I refer to my periods that require waiting. God isn't going to send us to the battlefield without wearing the garments of strength and wisdom. People are fickle at times and often want to steer us in the wrong direction. We must first make sure we have heard from God concerning our desires and requests. I am thankful we serve a God who has perfect timing. HE IS NEVER EARLY! HE IS NEVER LATE! HE IS ALWAYS ON TIME!

> *No one is good but One, that is, God. (Matthew 19:17)*

Thank you for your love to have us wait so you can prepare us for our mission in life. A good warrior never goes to battle without being properly trained!

Day 7

Eyes of Love

Thank you for seeing us through the eyes of love. You see our hearts when we go against your lead. There may be megafear, insecurity, or just wanting to be seen. Like Gideon, we may think we are too fragile to do what You are asking of us. Just because we know what we are truly made of does not mean You cannot take the least in stature or strength and anoint us to do miraculous things, not in our own strength but in Your anointed strength and God-given abilities.

I know God will never ask more of us than he knows we can do on his behalf. Sometimes I think my role in life is too mundane, or I don't seem to be doing enough for the kingdom. Just to mention his name to a lost person is seen as a great victory in God's eyes. Taking any opportunity afforded us to spread the gospel to the lost and unsaved is not seen as being unimportant to the kingdom of God. Giving a smile to a lonely and sad individual is seen as a good thing.

Sometimes when I am out, God may give me the urge to give someone a small amount of money. It might be a dollar bill, which is a meager amount, but to this person, it may mean they can now buy something to eat or ride the bus home. In serving, the Lord does not expect us to perform flamboyantly, have a best-selling novel, or win the Pulitzer Prize for Christianity. It may be as simple as a friendly hello to someone you walk by on the street. So don't allow the lying enemy to discourage you and give you a line of bull! Tell him to go away, that he is a stinking liar, and that you do not permit him to come anywhere near you or your family! He will flee at the mere mention of the mighty name of Jesus!

Often, when we least expect it, God will make it known to you that He is pleased with the smallest display of kindness or support you offered to a hurting friend. Always remember that He cares about our every issue, down to the smallest. What concerns us concerns Him just as much.

> *A new commandment I give*
> *to you, that you love one another;*
> *as I have loved you, that you also*
> *love one another. (John 13:34)*

Cast your cares upon His strong shoulders, and carry everything to Him in prayer.

Thank you, Lord, for lending us Your shoulders to cast our care upon.

Day 8

Seeing Our Hidden Qualities

Something I discovered about Jesus is that He knew exactly who He was getting when He chose me to be an ambassador for His kingdom. So there hasn't been anything I have done that has surprised Him.

Thank you, Lord, for seeing something in me that I had no idea was there. You pulled out qualities and attributes that only You could bring to the surface. Just like I tell people, if I had ever expected to look for every stain remover made to get my daughter's clothes spotlessly clean when I was in college doing the college scene, you would have thought of me to be off my rocker. But since becoming a parent, there have been certain qualities that have seeped out of me. Knowing my purpose was to raise and protect my offspring brought these deeply hidden qualities out into the open.

Our heavenly parent sees us as if these abilities have always been there; it's just that the moment and place have not arrived for them to fully manifest! Aren't you glad we have a God who teaches us and gives us the confidence, boldness, and tools to accomplish what is needed to get the glory? Praise His holy name!

> *For I know the plans I have*
> *for you declares the LORD, plans to*
> *prosper you and not to harm you,*
> *plans to give you hope and a future.*
> *(Jeremiah 29:11)*

> *For we are His workmanship,*
> *created in Christ Jesus for good*
> *works, which God prepared before-*
> *hand that we should walk in them.*
> *(Ephesians 2:10)*

Thank you for your nurturing and patient methods during our times of trial and error, training us to be mighty warriors. Qualities and abilities that only You saw have risen to the surface because of Your patience and abiding love.

Day 9

Strength Will Come

Have you ever been in a situation where you are asking yourself, "Where am I going to find the strength to get through this?" Well, let me tell you that through Christ, the strength will come in time. The strength you never dreamed you had will rise out of your heart. Remember, when life gets tough, the tough get going. Life can be so stressful when it seems as if all hell is rising against us. Just remember what the word says: "The gates of hell shall not prevail!" Christ will deliver His strength to see His child through this very difficult season. It may be financial, family oriented, or some situation arising from intentional and malicious insults on the part of someone you hold near and dear to your heart—situations orchestrated from the pits of hell. Demonic assignments cannot stop the plan of God. If it is ordained by the Lord above, nothing will stand in your way. Things may come up that delay you, but nothing can stop the plan of God from manifesting. "No weapon formed against me shall prosper."

Often, when situations arise, you ask yourself, Who is causing this turbulence in my life? All who love God hear his voice. If the words or thoughts in your mind make you feel bothered and confused, they are not coming from God; Satan is the author of confusion. Our Lord is a peaceful and calm God. He will bring it to pass. In my life, I have found strength I didn't realize I had, flowing from the fountain of God, who drenched us with His strength to fight what looks like such a huge mountain. Say to that mountain, "Be moved in Jesus' name," and watch to see the miracles of God take place right before your eyes. With God, all things are possible!

I can do all things through
Christ who strengthens me.
(Philippians 4:13)

Thank you, Lord, for giving me strength when I need it most.

Day 10

God Does Hear Our Prayers

Today, let's talk about when it seems as if our prayers aren't going any further than the ceiling! Sometimes, when nothing is happening in the natural, be assured that our Heavenly Father is working behind the scenes on our behalf! I have been there a few times, and suddenly, my prayers are answered, sometimes in the most unusual way. I sometimes have difficulty realizing that my prayers are being heard and answered in a way I did not think of myself.

His thoughts are higher than our thoughts, and His ways are higher than our ways as well. That is when our faith is tested almost to the brink of dismay. Just keep trusting that His promises are yes and amen. We need to speak words of faith as if our prayers have already been answered. Faith is the substance of things hoped for and the evidence of things not yet seen. In times like these, having faith can be almost impossible. It felt as if everything I had believed and lived for was going up in smoke. The enemy kept whispering, *"You are stuck, and the Lord has abandoned you."* Wrong!

I do believe He will never leave me or forsake me, no matter how it looks in the natural; He is definitely working things out in His way and in His timing. Remember, our Heavenly Father cares about our every concern. When it looks hopeless and that mountain you are now facing looks like it will never be moved, remember that God is in control. Letting go and allowing God to manifest His will and power in our lives can be a true test of our sincere faith in Him. It is there in the wilderness that we grow and flourish while growing closer to our God than ever before. Managing to give Him praise during our wilderness experience will guarantee He is planning to give us the desires of our hearts.

God is a loving and giving God who loves to give to His children just as we, as parents, love to give to our own children. Would we give our children, who are so precious to us, something that would bring heartache and destruction? As our children grow up, we, as parents, have been given the awesome responsibility of raising them in the admonition of our Lord. Children often ask for something that is simply impossible to give them. Our children cannot see the dangers ahead of them if we give them everything they ask for. In the same way, our Heavenly Father will not give us something that He knows all too well will be our demise and utterly devastate our lives.

Have you ever thanked Him for not answering your prayers as you had hoped? I look back and am truly grateful that He withheld from this child when not answering my prayers my way! Trust is the most important key to having a secure and peaceful existence. Give Him the highest praise when we are walking in the valley because, when the time is right, He will give us a glimpse of the plans he has so carefully mapped out for our lives! Put on a praise CD and get down to some honest and sincere praise to the God who loves us more than words could ever express!

> *Now this is the confidence that we have in Him, that if we ask anything according to His will, He hears us. And if we know that He hears us, whatever we ask, we know that we have the petitions that we have asked of Him. (1 John 5:14–15)*

Growing in Christ

What puzzles and utterly amazes me is when I look back to remember who I used to be before growing in the Lord. I have often said, "WHAT IN THIS WORLD WAS I THINKING ANYWAY?" The phrases, "I am a new creature in Christ" and "Old things have passed away" most definitely apply to me! How could I have ever been so blinded by the tricks of the enemy?

Children observe, model, and accept what they see in their homes. It causes their spiritual chemistry to be attracted to what is familiar, whether it is right or wrong! Changing our spiritual chemistry takes time and energy. Most of all, we must have a sincere desire to change. It was like blinders were lifted from my eyes! Life looked totally different, and I kept saying repeatedly, "I am the righteousness of Christ. I am a victor and not a victim!" Trying to make sense of situations that have arisen since walking hand in hand with Christ has often left me feeling exhausted and emotionally incapacitated. The most important lesson I did learn is that every word written for us to be instructed by is absolutely true! Fighting our spiritual battles using the weapons the Lord has shown us in the Word of God really does work, as we are victorious in our efforts to free ourselves from the tricks of the enemy! No doubt about that! No hesitation or reservation when declaring his strategies guarantees our success in stopping the assignments sent against us. It works in our favor every time!

We, as believers, have supreme authority to tread on serpents, crushing their heads like marshmallows! Glory to God! He wants us to win each battle and retain the victory that through him is ours, to mark it down as another victory and another milestone, to stack up as we knock out the plans our enemy had to kill, steal, destroy, and ultimately pull us away from God! The weapons of our warfare are not of carnal origin but are sent to us by the prince of the air. None of us are exempt from fighting the good fight sent our way when accepting Christ as our Lord and Savior! Our angels protect us from the fiery darts aimed toward us as if they were tiny picks.

Our worst day with Christ is better than our best day without him. An entire fleet of demons cannot defeat us when we use the spiritual authority given to us as followers of Christ.

I have just recently understood just how much Christ loves us, just how much power we possess if utilized when warring against the enemy, and just how Christ desires us to have a victorious life every day. Praise will repel the demons who attempt to destroy us or bring us heartache and discouragement, trying to discourage us to start doubting, possibly weakening our faith. Remain steadfast and hold on tightly to the Father's hand, and he will lead you to safety, taking us to higher grounds and higher levels of faith than ever before!

> *Therefore, if anyone is in Christ, he is a new creation; old things have passed away; behold, all things have become new. (2 Corinthians 5:17)*

Dear Lord, take me higher than I have ever risen before. Allow me to soar with the eagles, escaping our predators who relentlessly attempt to bring us down!

Day 12

Speak Cautiously

Have you ever been mistaken about the character and integrity of a so-called friend? If this so-called friend calls you and bad-mouthed one of their so-called friends, you better believe they will do the same thing to you. I ask myself, *Why did I ignore the warning signs?* I always give them the benefit of the doubt, ignorantly believing they are my best friend and just need someone to whom they can vent. WRONG! Beware of people like this. It usually breeds trouble, and naturally, we want to think they are trustworthy and that you are their best friend and confidant!

Over the years, I have learned many painful lessons about people who bad-mouth one of our so-called friends. Don't even think for a minute that you are the exception to the rule. I have dropped several so-called best friends for that very reason. We certainly do not need friends like these in our lives. Once the boundaries have been crossed, it takes a strong will to end a going-nowhere and unhealthy friendship such as this. Gossip is deadly and causes much confusion and heartache, especially when you realize you have been manipulated into thinking you are their best friend, and that they only need to share their intimate words with you and you alone.

Let me tell you about a friend who is assuredly trustworthy and shows the same love and equal treatment to everyone. The best friend we can ever have is Christ, who never gossips or betrays his children. Knowing that I give everyone a second chance has been used by the enemy against me. When I realize a relationship is draining me of my emotional energy, it is best for me to end it. I feel so much better now that I chose not to listen to anyone backbiting their family members and friends or even being negative about life in general.

I enabled so many unhealthy friendships over the years, and it took some hard self-control to end several of those types of dangerous friendships. I am blessed to know that I can have an ongoing friendship without worry or concern. Once I came to this realization, the blinders came off, and boy, was it ever freeing. When I am extremely lonely or very bored, I think about calling one of my dragon ex-friends, and then I choose to practice much self-control. Even though you really liked that person, you cannot allow yourself to become entangled again. Once you have closed that door, leave it closed permanently. God has so much more he wants you to experience, and he will give you good, trustworthy friends to add to your life.

> *A man who has friends must himself be friendly, but there is a friend who sticks closer than a brother. (Proverbs 18:24)*

Lord, thank you for being a friend who sticks closer than a brother. Thank you for being my very best friend.

Free from Fear

How many of us allow fear to rule us? Earlier today, when a close friend told me she has arthritis, I automatically began to fear that I, too, would develop it. As we talked, she told me that there was a need for me to have a bone density test done. I felt such a wave of fear go through me; it was almost paralyzing. As we discussed her symptoms, it occurred to me that everything she said related to me. I had to literally take total control of my thoughts and the direction they were headed. How easy it is to slip into fear mode without even realizing it. I may have creaky bones and stiff joints, but there is absolutely no way it could be arthritis. What if it were? Would having arthritis be the worst thing in the world?

The enemy simply enjoys it when we start thinking and begin to enter a fear mindset! There is nothing to fear but fear itself. When we rely on God as our source, there is nothing he cannot handle. Together, we can handle any problem that arises. Then I asked God to give me peace and told myself it was wasted emotional energy to start worrying about something without proof or reason. Our fears can lead us to do certain things we wouldn't ordinarily do. Having the right type of fear where we use precautionary measures helps us remain safe and think rationally. We certainly would not step on a railroad track without looking both ways before venturing to cross the tracks. We need to take care of our bodies and take preventative measures by having annual checkups and preventative procedures to make sure that we are cancer-free, that our blood pressure is normal, and to keep a check on any unwanted pounds.

Fear, used with wisdom, can keep us alive longer. However, taking fear just a little too far can be cumbersome and emotionally exhausting. Do we carry an umbrella when there isn't a cloud in the sky just because we fear it will rain? Who wants to lug an umbrella around when the sunshine is predominantly capturing the skies? If the weather forecast predicts a 70 percent chance of rain, then it is wise to bring an umbrella along. When fear grips us unreasonably, we need to start trusting God with our tomorrows, knowing that whatever it brings will give us a sigh of relief and a sense of peace. For no matter what happens in our tomorrows, God will be there to walk with us through the storms of life.

> *So do not fear, for I am with you; do not be dismayed, for I am your God. I will strengthen you and help you; I will uphold you with my righteous right hand. (Isaiah 41:10)*

Thank you, Lord, for always being there for me, no matter what is taking place in my life; I can draw strength from you, which allows me to create a fearless existence.

Day 14

Our Beautiful World

This morning, when taking my dogs outside for their morning appointment in the backyard, a thought came to me about how beautifully God created our world. The trees and flowers all know when to bloom and blossom, as if they were programmed to do so by our awesome God. The flowers seem to know the season to bloom and when it is time to stop blooming; and when you stop to consider just how marvelous the ecosystem is, well, it is totally overwhelming. With a spoken word, our God caused the dark to turn to light and the mountains to stand tall above the beautiful surroundings graced with grass, flowers, and smaller trees. When the earth was finished and complete with human beings, the Lord stepped back and knew he had done a good thing—an outstanding job! I truly agree, don't you?

Have you ever wondered who created God? Does He have anyone to answer to, or is He an omni-present being? I adore Him so much. It is impossible to even fathom life without His abiding presence! I think it is important to take time to take in such an awesome beauty around us. For me, flowers are my favorite objects to see. For someone like me, growing flowers is hard since I do not possess the gift of having them flourish. Some people have the natural ability to take a sand pile and grow fantastic sand flowers! I am so grateful to have the privilege to gaze upon such natural wonders as the majestic mountains and breathtaking views seen when standing on the top of a gloriously formed mountain.

Our national parks reflect their natural beauty, and to me, seeing the different types of clouds rising high above us gives me such a feeling of peace. When the sky is still and all is well in the universe, it thrills me. Even when it does rain and our fluffy clouds turn dark and start shifting our way, I don't fear a storm, for our earth needs to be watered. Think of the mind that was intelligent enough to create everything in our world yet has the time to listen to our prayers and assuredly cares about our every concern. Praise to the

Lord of lords, the creator of our awesome world. So let's give Him all the glory, for He is to be honored!

> *In the beginning, God created the heavens and the earth. (Genesis 1:1)*

> *The heavens declare the glory of God; and the firmament shows His handiwork. (Psalm 19:1)*

Lord, thank you for speaking our beautiful world into existence and allowing us to bask in the glory and splendor all around us.

Day 15

Waiting Is an Action

Do you realize waiting is an action? Perhaps you think that simply because you are not doing anything during the interim, you aren't doing anything. It is much easier to wait when we know what we are waiting for. Be confident that God is working behind the scenes on our behalf. Are you asking for a breakthrough in your family, strongholds to come down, a better-paying job, or someone to conquer addiction? I have learned that praising Him during the waiting season, which sometimes seems like an eternity, is the action needed. When we least expect it, our waiting comes to an end. It takes preparation time for our prayers to be answered, and God is merely getting us ready for the next level. So if you have been waiting for what seems like forever, don't give up! If your prayers have not been answered, then there is a very good reason. Just sit tight and wait on him to come through for you. God knows what is best for us when we don't have a clue of what we think we wanted. What we are asking for may very well be harmful to us. There may be a better plan just waiting to unfold.

> *But they that wait upon the* LORD *shall renew their strength; they shall mount up with wings as eagles; they shall run, and not be weary; they shall walk, and not faint. (Isaiah 40:31)*

> *Wait on the Lord; be of good courage, and He shall strengthen your heart. Wait, I say, on the Lord! (Psalm 27:14)*

Lord, help me to wait, and while I wait, give me peace and joy that only You can supply.

Day 16

Being Chosen

Lord, thank you for choosing me even though you knew my many imperfections. You saw something that only you could see and qualities that I had no idea would unfold. When I think about the many mistakes and poor choices I have made over the years, it causes me to marvel at just thinking about your unconditional love.

The enemy loves to remind us of our many serious blunders, whether they were done intentionally or out of total innocence and trusting the wrong people. It suddenly occurred to me that I saw everyone behind these rose-colored glasses. I thought everyone was like me, and it tripped me out when I found out through some very painful and hard lessons that people are not like me. People often pretend to be one way, but eventually, their true colors are revealed. Being so blatantly honest about who I am has cost me a lot! I trust people until they give me a reason not to; but even then, I always want to give them the benefit of the doubt. Why do we do this? It could be because you grew up in an environment that was not safe, or maybe your parents were not trustworthy. Just because they are our parents doesn't always mean they will make the best decisions on our behalf.

Finally, I have grasped the fact that God loves me completely, even down to my numerous faults and shortcomings. God sees our hearts and knows more than anyone else what we are made of. Once we surrender our hearts and lives to him without reservation—I MEAN, GIVING EVERYTHING TO GOD—our thought process will change, and we will begin to see life the way it is. Have you ever noticed the heroes in the Bible who have gone through some very turbulent experiences? They trusted God, and He came through for each one in a mighty way. God is God, and with Him, nothing is impossible.

For many are called, but few
are chosen. (Matthew 22:14)

Lord, I believe You can move mountains in our way. Waiting for You to work Your miracles in our daily lives is what keeps us desiring to grow closer to You every day.

Day 17

God's Timing

When I awoke this morning, I knew I needed to thank the Lord for His timing! It is very difficult to endure the waiting, even though I know that the plan the Lord has for my life will be the very best. I do not possess the ability to orchestrate the marvelous plan the Lord has already begun to bring forth. In His sovereignty and wisdom, He always knows what is best for His children, just as every parent usually knows what is best for their children. As children in the kingdom of God, we are not wise enough to see the big picture, and what we think is the best may not be. God sees the entire picture and has the authority to manifest it.

Lord, give me the patience I will need to see this waiting season to its completion!

As I wait, my flesh burns, and a part of me wants to scream out, "LET ME HAVE MY WAY!" Often, giving us our way is not the safest thing for God to do. Persistence when approaching the throne of grace with our requests may cause Him to go ahead and give it to us our way. I am choosing to wait to get the answers and results that God desires. I hope that in my many years of following my Lord, I have gained a little wisdom and have the courage and fortitude to wait it out. I would rather wait than wish I had waited. Even though I have trouble with trust issues, I have grown to trust my Heavenly Father more than I could ever trust my earthly father.

When it seems as if nothing is happening the way we want it, we may think that God has forgotten us. That's not the case. In fact, it is when we feel like our prayers only went to the ceiling of our kitchen that the Lord is really on the ball. It takes time to accurately orchestrate and map out the divine plan and purpose for our lives. In the meantime, I am choosing to praise Him and enjoy the joy of the Lord.

Do you remember the song we sang when we were just small children? "I've got the joy, joy, joy, joy down in my heart, down in my heart, down in my heart. I've got the joy, joy, joy, joy down in my heart, down in my heart to stay!" I am so happy, so very happy that I have the love of Jesus in my heart!

> *You will show me the path of*
> *life; in Your presence is fullness of*
> *joy; in your right hand are plea-*
> *sures forevermore. (Psalm 16:11)*

Thank you for the joy of the Lord that is in my heart! Trusting in your plan brings me joy and peace.

Day 18

Feeling Lonely

Do you feel lonely in a crowded room? What about when you are home alone?

When I feel lonely, I start talking to God. I have often asked Him to send me a mate. Would that fill the void? Not entirely, because without God, we will always need to feel the presence of the Holy One! No man or person can fill the void that only God can fill. I do hope you never feel as lonely as I do at times.

Several years ago, I went to the altar to have my pastor pray for me, and then I started praying in my private and very personal prayer language. Well, unknown to me, he interpreted it as the Bible states it must be done. His words shocked me! He told me I was telling God I was afraid of being alone. He then asked for a prayer cloth to cover my head. Then he proceeded to tell me the cloth represented God, who was always with me. From that point on, I have purposely remembered that God is going to be with me forever. He will never leave me or forsake me! What a glorious thing to know, especially when you are single. I then felt better and am thankful for His sweet presence.

Earlier in my life, I was very independent, and being home alone in the house truly never bothered me in the least. I have friends who must be married to feel complete. I am a whole person, with or without a helpmate. Even so, when God does give me a life mate to walk this path together, I will never forsake my Lord, who carried me through many lonely nights! I love my Lord, and no one could ever replace Him. Spending time with my Heavenly Father completes me. Many people turn to God only in times of turmoil, or, in other words, when they need something from Him. I am thankful He is with me from morning to night and protects me during the night while I sleep. I want to be the type of Christian who acknowledges what God has done for me. I appreciate Him more than words could ever express.

During the quiet moments around my house, I bask in his presence, and we share quality time together. God speaks to me in the stillness of the moment. He will speak to you during your quiet moment—that is, if, around your busy house, there are quiet moments.

> *Be strong and courageous. Do not be afraid or terrified because of them, for the Lord your God goes with you; he will never leave your nor forsake you. (Deuteronomy 31:6)*

Thank You for Your abiding presence and the talks we have when all is still, and I can hear very clearly Your words of comfort and love.

Day 19

Passing the Test

One day, as I was going through yet another test sent to me by God, the cashier from a local store gave me several pennies too much in change, and honestly, I was tempted to keep them for a rainy day. But then I told God I would take them back tomorrow because it looked like it was going to rain any minute now. The urging of the Holy Spirit tugged at my heart, and then I asked him if I had to turn around and walk all the way back to the store just to return several pennies. His reply was, "Of course, you do." Before I could blink an eye, I had pivoted around and headed back to return the pennies. The cashier looked per-plexed when I came back to give him the pennies. He wasn't accustomed to anyone being so honest or caring enough to walk back just to give back a few pennies!

I know God was testing me, and it states in the Word of God that if He can trust us in the little things, He can trust us with larger things. I definitely want to pass the test! I am tested often and know, without any doubt, that God is preparing me to prosper financially! So passing every test is vitally important; even the small tests must not go unnoticed.

My heart hurts when I think I have failed one of my many tests, whether it is about money or just being totally honest. Sometimes, it seems the world we live in today has become desensitized to sin without a single tug at the heart or the slightest conviction. I will always appreciate the tests I am given and want to pass every one of them with flying colors! How can we claim to love God and then turn around and lie about something or steal from our neighbors when no one is looking, even if we know we can get away with it?

> *His master replied, "Well done, good and faithful servant! You have been faithful with a few things; I will put you in charge of many things. Come and share your master's happiness!" (Matthew 25:23)*

The more I know about my God, the more I strive to please Him; He is pleased when His children obey Him and act according to His bidding.

Day 20

Taking Care of Ourselves

Taking care of ourselves can be tough, especially if your role model did not take care of themselves. Somehow, we learned martyrdom by watching our parental role models. Truthfully, I will never be a Joan of Arc! Many times I have mistaken the verse in the Bible for having the means to meet the need of someone who is in need—if your brother thirsts, then give him a cool drink of water; if your sister is hungry, then give her something to eat. Saying that doesn't mean everyone and every time. I am not saying not to help or share your blessings by quenching someone's thirst or sharing your nourishment with a fellow human being. What I finally had to come to terms with was that many people are always in need, always thirsty, and always hungry! Taking this verse literally has put me in some very awkward situations.

Several years ago, when going through a serious illness and having a lengthy recuperation period, I began to feel drained and totally empty. The people who had basically used me as a crutch did not let up for one minute. It was then that I realized it was okay to take care of myself emotionally. This revelation led me to end some so-called friendships. I am certain these emotionally draining people did not waste time finding another stool pigeon to suck the life out of! What is even sadder is that a few of them were family members! To my utter amazement, I had been enabling them, and I didn't have a clue. I, or we, thought I was being a good friend to these apparently needy folks. WRONG!

I have then categorized people into an *us* or a *them*. Seeing myself as being an *us* without a doubt was constantly comforting to someone who felt victimized and simply refused to even attempt to change. Well, eventually seeing this, I had to make this vitally important decision to STOP enabling, or better yet, stop allowing these cunning and manipulative people to get one over on me. It totally freed me from feeling guilty for not returning the fifth phone call from the same people in only several hours. What about giving them money, only to find out their spending habits need some serious improvement or upgrading? Maybe if they did not waste so much money on foolishness, they would have money rather than being broke all the time. The saddest part of my many years of enabling or extreme codependence is when I discovered they could make it without my help.

I have since been delivered from codependency, and the blinders are gone from my eyes. What I see now is a clear picture of people who have the job of squeezing the life out of anyone they can! One of the most difficult areas of holdback is with my grown, married children and my precious grandchildren. Actually, they are happier when I leave their problems for them to deal with. I have such a soft spot in my big heart for my family, but even family members can be emotionally draining. Finally, God showed me the errors of my ways.

God allows us to go through situations in our lives without lending a hand, except to hear our prayers and send us to the wilderness, where we flourish, grow closer, and become radical followers of him.

Above all else, guard your heart, for everything you do flows from it. (Proverbs 4:23)

I thank you, Lord, for loving me enough to chastise me and for gently giving me the truth about having an unhealthy enabling habit. Tough love to the max is what must be demonstrated, which is the greatest kind of love for the benefit of everyone involved.

Being Content

Have you ever found yourself wishing for something other than what is happening in your life right now? As we struggle to find our purpose, it gets tiring. Even Christ prayed for some other way to fulfill His divine purpose rather than dying on the rugged and cruel cross. When our purpose seems to be taking forever to manifest, we get impatient and grow weary. Christ undoubtedly knew His purpose for coming to earth to live among mankind. He went about doing His Father's business by preaching the gospel. He healed the blind man; He cast out demons, sending them to drown in the river. Are we certain we haven't found our purpose?

I believe that during the waiting time, we can share the gospel, have a joyful heart, and sing his praises! Sometimes, fulfilling our purpose is different from what we thought it was. It could be that we are only meant to share the good news or spread some hope and joy of the Lord to the lost and dying world. People see something in us they want but may not know how to receive it. Many unsaved people may see what we have and want it, and yet they have never been shown the way to have it working in their personal life.

When I found myself in certain situations, I learned to ask God what I could do to glorify him. One time several years ago, I had no other choice but to utilize the local laundromat, which I absolutely did not enjoy, but I chose to use that time to place gospel tracts between the pages of magazines set out for patrons to read or fumble through. I then watched people flipping through the pages of a magazine of their choice and watching a tract fall out. Many stopped to read the words that explained the plan of salvation. Even a glance was often enough to stir up their interest. It thrilled my heart to see people reading them. Then sometimes, I managed to start up a conversation about Christ, which I thoroughly enjoyed! I was pleasantly surprised to find out most people were eager to hear about the miracles I had experienced myself. Then on other days, I couldn't seem to even get a hello out of anyone. I decided to spend those boring days in the laundromat, witnessing wherever possible. When my mission was complete, God allowed me to get my own washer and dryer.

It doesn't matter where we are or what we are going through; we can have a purpose. It may not be the ultimate purpose designed for us, but at least we did accomplish our goal by witnessing to people. I had to purposely come up with creative ideas to do such as the tracts in the magazine. Perhaps just a friendly smile to a passerby will give them hope of a better day. Christ did die on the cross for our sins and rose again to take the keys to the kingdom away from the enemy and proclaim a marvelous and thrilling victory! Our deeds may not be seen by anyone except God, but each thing done in some small way is just as important to the kingdom as a crusade might be. Reaching people where they are is what is important. So be ready; you could be asked to witness. Oh, and be on guard to take the opportunities provided, no matter where we are!

I am not saying this because
I am in need, for I have learned to

*be content whatever the circum-
stances. (Philippians 4:11)*

Lord, give me the courage to wait with peace and joy and to just be satisfied to offer the message anywhere to anyone willing to listen.

Why Worry?

Do you find yourself worrying or feeling guilty? According to Dr. Wayne Dyer, worry and guilt are futile emotions. I don't want to worry, but I am a planner, and if my plans are not carried out to my specification, then I worry! Worry drains us of energy and time. Knowing that God is in control doesn't always prevent us from worrying, does it? God created us in our humanness and even told us not to fret, but in all situations, be content. It is a waste of time and energy to worry.

Sometimes I worry about every scenario known to man. I even tell God it is just that I love my family so much and that trying to prevent any harm coming to them has to make worrying acceptable; but no, it isn't acceptable at all. If I think of every possible negative event that might take place, then when it doesn't happen, I am relieved. I know how precious life is and how quickly it can be gone without a moment's notice.

When I sin against God, I am so guilt ridden, but guilt is such a wasted emotion and very exhausting as well. The enemy enjoys putting thoughts in our heads to cause us to worry or feel guilty. There is no condemnation in the kingdom of God. He paid the ultimate price when he died on the cross. Life will happen no matter how much we worry about issues.

Being someone who thinks too much, it is very difficult for me to stop worrying or feeling guilty when it begins. Casting down vain imaginations is a very true statement, and as Christians, we must trust, realizing that no matter what happens to us, our Lord will see us through. Leaning on him will offer support during trying times and painful situations. I put forth much effort to put these emotions aside, especially when out in the public eye. It is part of the mask we wear to fool our friends and make them think we don't have a care in the world. I am not implying we don't take precautions when it comes to our loved ones, such as sending your child out on a stormy morning and making sure he has an umbrella or a waterproof jacket. That isn't the type of worry I am referring to.

I feel guilty when I think I have let someone down, but sometimes, we cannot live up to unfair expectations placed on us by others. It may be called conviction that streams from our heart if we have sinned against our Lord. We are not responsible for the overall well-being of everyone who crosses our path. Be punctual and know that, to get to work on time, leaving thirty minutes early to avoid the traffic is a good way to make sure you arrive on time. Take inventory of what type of things you are worrying about or what are you feeling guilty about. Life is hectic, but adding these energy-zapping emotions only wears us out and doesn't help us at all. Just place your future in the capable hands of God, and remember Lot's wife when she looked back and turned into a pillar of salt. The past is gone, and all we have is today. So live it to the fullest and enjoy your journey. The days slip away so rapidly, and living each day worry- and guilt-free will allow us to enjoy our journey. Our future is bright and promising.

Therefore do not worry about
tomorrow, for tomorrow will worry

about itself Each day has enough
trouble of its own. (Matthew 6:34)

Lord, help me place everything in your care and realize that worry and guilt only steal my joy today.

Day 23

Fearless Living

FEAR! Yes, I said fear. Fear is the one demon spirit that plagues each one of us at one point or another. It sneaks in and grips us—fear of being alone, deprivation, rejection, and many other things. Having some anticipatory fear is normal. When we do something we haven't done before, of course, there is a little fear that comes. It's the fear of not knowing what to expect or how it works in our new adventure. It is normal to feel that type of fear, but allowing it to grip you until you are paralyzed is not. We must learn to recognize that type of fear slipping into our subconscious and take inventory. When fear is prevalent in your life, it is time to take control of it.

A number of fears are defined for us—fear of being in closed spaces, fear of insects, fear of being alone, fear of heights, fear of dying, fear of losing a loved one, fear of success, and fear of being different and not being accepted for who we are. I can mention several more, but listing them is not necessary for you to get the picture. True fear is the absence of God in your life. Faith is doing what you fear and knowing God is with you and will help you get through it.

As a young child, I was much braver about doing risky things than I am now in my golden years. Why? We realize what might happen and want to prevent it from happening if possible. There have been times when fear gripped me so strongly that I made decisions out of fear. Usually, these decisions were disastrous, and later, I understood what led me to make such blatantly destructive decisions. When we allow God into every part of our daily lives, he will keep us from experiencing such extreme fear. Having faith the size of a mustard seed is all that is required, but do we always include God in this equation, especially when we know God has called us for a particular task and the enemy comes against us ferociously and fear begins to slip in?

Shake it off, and if you must do it feeling afraid, go ahead and get it done and just watch how God will soothe your fears. Things always work out when God has called us and anointed us for the job! False evidence appearing real can put us in some very awkward situations. It is not an easy thing to do something with trembling and fear, but we can do all things through Christ who strengthens us.

> *For God hath not given us*
> *the spirit of fear; but of power, and*
> *of love, and of a sound mind. (2*
> *Timothy 1:7)*

I thank you, Lord, for the strength to accomplish Your purpose, even when we feel fearful. Faith and God will be the best way to accomplish Your purpose for my life.

Healing a Broken Heart

Hurting people hurt people! What saddens me is that these people don't even know they are hurting others. They are living as wounded people who have no clue why they hurt so much. Their hearts have been bruised and battered, so out of the heart, we speak or act. Determining the causation factors that control hurting people to the point they lash out at everyone around them can be a very confusing matter.

As adults, we develop some type of self-preservation mechanism to numb the hurt and pain. Perhaps it originated from childhood, a failed marriage, or betrayal. It is easier said than done to give your hurts and brokenness to Christ, especially when we haven't come to terms with other issues. Jesus came to heal the brokenhearted and give us hope and comfort.

Many folks appear not to have a care in the world. Behind the mask lie pain and brokenness. Putting on a public face is accepted; we certainly wouldn't want to expose our hearts to everyone!

Just lately, a friend from my church and I began to warm up to each other. We have known each other for many years, but it was never more than a friendly greeting. I know that God put us together for the season both of us are in. We offered each other what was needed to see us through the storms of our lives. God always gives us exactly what we need before we even realize we need it.

All of us have met people who walk around taking out their pain and hurt on those who attempt to befriend them. As we grow and mature in the Lord, he will allow us to be exposed to our issues, just like peeling an onion—one thin layer at a time. God is a God of compassion, and if our issues were exposed to us all at once, it would probably blow our minds. Discovering the core roots of our brokenness can be cumbersome, but we must relentlessly pursue the search for a solution, that is, if we really desire to be healed! With persistence and long-suffering, eventually the answers will begin to surface.

Many people never make it to true healing while continuing to fake it for appearance's sake. Christ will heal us if we turn it over to Him. I have never known a single person free of pain and heartache, unless they are like a stone without feelings or emotions. Being a behaviorist, I have always tried to step back and make some unprofessional assessment regarding certain behaviors demonstrated or words spoken to give them the benefit of the doubt. Basically, as human beings, we want the same things: to be loved, accepted, have friendships, and live cohesively with one another.

Dealing with pain and hurt will motivate people to say hurtful things and act strangely for protection's sake. Jesus does understand the pain and hurt experienced by human beings, for He felt the same emotions of betrayal and rejection! Those who hurt us with unkind words or rude actions need the love of Christ to engulf their brokenness. Learning to love this type of individual can be extremely difficult, and it may often appear as if it is a hopeless venture on our part. I am very thankful God took the time to look past my words and actions to see something in me no one had ever taken the time to recognize!

The Lord is near to those who
have a broken heart. And He saves

those who are broken in spirit.
(Psalm 34:18)

Lord of mercy, how I appreciate you for seeing me for the person I longed to be. Once I managed to move past and rise above my brokenness, it was then that the healing began. Praise Your holy name!

Day 25

God's Abundant Grace

Have you ever taken time to think about the awesome gift of grace? Grace is always present for those who believe. Without grace, our lives would be a mess! God's grace is such a valuable commodity. Grace is never to be taken for granted. He gives us such abundant grace and demonstrates it in large doses. He chooses to see us through any situation we are facing.

Life can be cumbersome and perplexing at times. Knowing we have grace is comforting to me. I am not talking about doing anything and everything that sins against our God and then expecting to have it go unnoticed. We will reap the consequences of our actions. It is when we realize the outcome of our sin that grace steps in to see us through our mess—grace so rich and free it cannot be adequately described.

First, repentance needs to take place—not phony repentance but sincere remorse for our acts of sin. Sin is missing the mark. As humans, we often cannot stop sinning without the grace of our Lord. The seriousness of our need to find grace cannot be measured. It is when we purposely go against the bidding of God for whatever reason that we truly understand grace. We are not supposed to get away with sinning and then think we are not going to suffer for our actions. Grace is given in the quantity needed for the specific circumstances.

God does possess the ability to reverse our sins, and He is always more than willing to welcome us back. If our hearts are changed, it seems to me that there can be no other way but to repent and start over. God, by no means, expects us to be perfect; he knew our nature when he created us in his image. Our justifications may cause us to avoid the truth of admitting we have sinned and come short of the glory of God. Often, we must endure these consequences until they have been transformed; and for those who love the Lord, it will happen in one way or another.

We must work out our salvation with fear and trembling. There are factors to think about in this formula. Many of us have grown up in dysfunctional families. Who hasn't? For us, dysfunction is all we know, and the customs we learned as children may cause us to sin without comprehending the nature of our actions. As we learn to trust in the ways of our Lord, we begin a transformation period. I have noticed so many changes in myself since truly surrendering my life to Him. People think that those of us who attend church regularly are saints, and they do not understand that just because we go to church doesn't mean we're perfect. We are sinners saved by grace. The beauty in it is when you start to notice the changes in yourself and then in others.

Grace is sufficient enough to allow the freedom to change. For me, it was like having someone raise the blinders off my eyes when I completely understood the nature of my dysfunctionality, not to excuse it but to conquer the beast within. Have you ever heard someone say, "That was just the way I was raised"? Keep in mind that that doesn't make it all right or acceptable, but it enters into our frame of reference. As we grow closer to the Lord and our sin nature conforms to the nature of God, grace is the most valuable gift given to followers of Christ.

And he said unto me, My
grace is sufficient for thee: for my

strength is made perfect in weakness. Most gladly therefore will I rather glory in my infirmities, that the power of Christ may rest upon me. (2 Corinthians 12:9)

As I walk with You daily, Lord, thank You for the grace to change and admit when I have failed you. Your grace is always sufficient.

Day 26

Dying to the Flesh

Worshipping the Lord doesn't only happen on Sundays! Walking with him daily is the most wonderful thing—taking him everywhere you go, not just when someone is looking. God sees us no matter where we are or what we are doing. It should matter more to us what God thinks than what our neighbors think. I feel a gentle tugging at my heart that cannot be coming from anywhere else but from the Holy Spirit.

I personally get upset with myself when I mess up and feel as if I have grieved the Holy Spirit. Sometimes I operate out of what I commonly refer to as my issue stupors; it is like something goes off inside my head, and I know I am acting out of my flesh. I know that, as Christians, we must die to the flesh, and for me, I have been a Christian long enough to be separated from the flesh. When we react out of our issue stupors and don't utilize the spiritual remedy for our actions, we are convicted. I know full well that my words or deeds are not coming from the right source, yet I do them anyway. Later, the feeling of sadness comes over me, and immediately, I start asking God to forgive me. At least now I know the source of such things.

It is difficult to let go of every hidden emotion that stems from our issue stupors. Often, I don't even acknowledge these issues. When time allows us to expose the ugly and dark issues that have haunted us for so long, do we mask them with some type of addiction? I chose codependency because it is less noticeable to anyone but me. In the long run, I suffered many emotional hardships.

I had a preacher many years ago who always said, "JUST GIVE IT TO JESUS, SISTER, AND LET IT GO." Did he not realize it may not be as simple as that? Letting go of unhealthy habits can be very complicated. First, identify them, confront them, and ask God to help you do whatever is necessary to change them. Will it happen overnight? No way! I have been working on mine for many years and still shock myself when certain situations arise. I think, *Where on earth did that come from?* It is a daily struggle to leave them far behind us. I may not be where I would like to be, but at least I am not where I used to be.

> *For if you live according to the flesh you will die; but if by the Spirit you put to death the deeds of the body, you will live. (Romans 8:13)*

Lord, help me rid myself of these issue stupors that interfere with my Christian walk and may hurt my witness. Thank you for your unconditional love and patience as I struggle to be the Christian you have called me to be.

Day 27

Walk in Love

Have you ever thought life is getting too complicated to endure? When things come against us in our daily lives, do we get mad or upset, rant, and rave about how unfair life can be? Yes, life can be very unfair at times. People lie, cheat, steal, and gossip. How do we deal with this? At first, we may react foolishly and speak out of our carnal nature. Do we stop and remember who is behind this unpleasant situation? Sometimes, life just happens, but then again, we may be reaping the consequences of our thoughtless words or actions.

I remember years ago when everyone rushed out to buy a WWJD bracelet. Now there is a new one: FROG—*fully rely on God*! I want to know exactly what Jesus would do if this had happened to Him.

Well, we witnessed meekness, which is power under control. When He was nailed to the cross, He could have called down angels and destroyed His accusers, but did He? No, He knew that His purpose and mission were completed by His ability to remain steadfast while accomplishing the ultimate sacrifice.

Asking yourself just what Jesus would have done or learning to fully rely on God applies to any situation. Taking a walk while talking to God about our cares will do wonders! It doesn't change the unfair deeds taken against us, but it will certainly soothe your wounded soul. Jesus knew about unfairness and experienced the same emotions we do. Can you imagine the heartache of betrayal by one of His own disciples? These unstable men suffered the consequences of their actions. I would hate to think how Jesus felt. Did he lose His cool, rant and rave, throw things, and get upset? No, in fact, He demonstrated power under control to the max and much wisdom when He treated them with kindness. How sad, for they once had been His friends, and now they became an opponent.

Will we ever get to that point in our daily walk with Christ to act out of our spirit man, or will we always get into the issue stupors? I disappoint myself, thinking that by now, having been a Christian for most of my life, I should be able to act as Christ did. The Lord truly understands our carnal and very human nature; after all, he created us.

> *Therefore be imitators of God as dear children. And walk in love, as Christ has also loved us and given himself for us, an offering and a sacrifice to God for a sweet-smelling aroma. (Ephesians 5:1–2)*

Lord, I give you praise and glory for showing me a much better way to respond when life is not fair. Your gentle spirit shows me I do not have to get upset or act out of my issue stupors. I want to please You more than I want to please the flesh.

Receive Your Radical Blessings

Do you find yourself sabotaging your blessings? Some of us have grown accustomed to having absolutely nothing. When blessings arrive, we don't exactly know how to receive them. The Lord has blessed me so abundantly, but for some reason, I always seem to detour them or totally sabotage my blessings. One morning in early December, the Lord spoke to me and told me His blessings were going to chase me down! Learning to graciously receive His blessings for me took some work.

Our flesh rebels when we are not used to being blessed in such abundance. That is called *afterburn*! Afterburn is when we have managed to change our behaviors, and our flesh and psyche burn to resist the change. The Lord then told me to get accustomed to receiving his radical blessings! My life is blessed beyond measure. Changing our natural response and the desire to do so takes time. There was a time in my life when guilt, shame, and self-condemnation owned me. It was just a major issue stupor taking charge of everything. Once I identified it, I had the task of confronting it. Now the hard part came as I began to struggle to change my unhealthy behaviors and learn to accept the grace, mercy, and fabulous blessings God has so richly bestowed upon me and my beloved family.

Guilt clouds your mind, shame wears us down like manual labor, and self-condemnation is not of God. It felt strange for a long time, and now I refuse to go back to my old ways. Christ came for mankind to give us the opportunity to choose His gift of salvation and everything associated with His gift. He ate with sinners, opened blind eyes, and caused the lame to walk again. So why would we allow ourselves to wallow in guilt, shame, and self-condemnation?

Believing in Christ gives us the power and authority to rise above our circumstances. He desires us to have what he died to give us—the freedom from guilt and shame and, more importantly, to finally experience deliverance from self-condemna-tion. We do this by casting down vain imaginations when the enemy tries to enter our thought life and taking authority over the tricks of the enemy when he tries to bring those futile emotions back on us. Unworthiness is the one feeling I had the hardest time ridding myself of. The enemy will try to tell us that because of our past sins, we are not worthy to receive these blessings or have freedom from these self-sabotaging behaviors! WRONG! We can take authority over these troubling and emotionally draining fiery darts shot at us by the enemy. Often, I remind the enemy he is a defeated foe and ask him why he even bothers trying to come against me when he knows I have the ultimate victory!

> *He redeemed us in order that the blessing given to Abraham might come to the Gentiles through Christ Jesus so that by faith we might receive the promise of the Spirit. (Galatians 3:14)*

Lord, I thank You for the freedom we have in Your name and the power and authority to live above our feelings that may stifle the glorious and joyful life You died to provide us.

Judge Not

Have you ever been judged incorrectly? Just recently, a woman I have gone to church with for seventeen years told me, "People just don't take the time to get to know you." I took that statement as a compliment. She went on to say, "I did not know what I was missing by not taking the time to get to know you sooner." I have no idea what she had thought of me before we became close friends.

How often do we form an opinion about someone based on their looks, eye color, weight, height, or ethnic origin, or just not give them a chance? Maybe this person doesn't live in the right neighborhood or have the same educational level as me. Aren't you thrilled that Jesus does not judge us by certain eligibility criteria?

Over the years, I have learned not to judge a book by its cover alone. People are marvelous creatures and worth taking a closer look at, looking past their looks or how they dress. Everyone, at some point or another, has based their overall opinion on their first impression. My pastor says if you come in the best clothes you have, then come on in.

I invited an acquaintance to come to church with me. I was shocked at her response as she began telling me she did not have nice enough clothing to come to my church. Jesus tells us to come as we are! He definitely knew what He was getting when He chose me to follow him. It doesn't matter to Christ what is worn on the outside; it's what is in our hearts that counts. Reaching out to those who are not like us, or what we think is acceptable, can cost us a lasting and worthwhile friendship. Aren't you grateful that Jesus did not look at our outward appearance or our outward actions?

There are many self-preservation mechanisms manifested by people that may cause us to hesitate to make friends with them. The need to survive is very strong among humans, and if we take the time to get to know them, it may help us understand them.

People misjudged Jesus based on His appearance. Without hearing Him preach, we would have missed out on the best storyteller ever. Jesus used parables to make a point, which have been repeated many times over the years!

I have often thought about how adventurous it would be to wear some funky hats and outlandish clothing or dye my hair pink! Would it make a difference just because people dress differently to make a statement about their uniqueness or individuality? Would it be difficult for me to feel totally comfortable about approaching someone dressed out of sync with the rest of the crowd? Why do we shy away from someone who is different? It blows my mind to discover that a person I stayed away from was seen by many as being very popular and likable. Everyone was created with their own set of fingerprints, which makes them stand out alone, and no one has the same set, which makes each person unique! However, there are common denominators all of us share—the need for a savior, the need to be loved, and the need for us to have our basic needs met.

When we choose to follow Christ, it says we are to be separated from this world. Even wearing a smile all the time might be seen as out of the ordinary. Does your opinion change when the person you avoided getting to know changes? When they show up at a reunion looking beautiful, when they were viewed as plain-looking in high school? They no longer wear glasses but are prosperous now, but they were viewed as a lower class back when you knew them in high school. Or did they marry a professional person, and then your opinion started to change?

In the kingdom of Christ, all people are treated exactly the same. God is no respecter of persons, and what he will do for one, he will also do for the person who may not smell good, for the person who wears ratty clothing, or for the person who might have no other choice but to live in substandard housing. There is a wonderful story behind each outward person projected by the person viewed as an outcast or unsociable. Jesus was bold in his ministry, often hanging out with those seen as unacceptable to society.

I am so excited to say that Jesus definitely looked deep into my heart and soul. If I had been judged by one of the qualities society did not accept, I would have been left out.

> *Do not judge, or you too will be judged. For in the same way you judge others, you will be judged, and with the measure you use, it will be measured to you. (Matthew 7:1–2)*

Thank you, Lord, for taking the time to see something in me the world may have seen as unacceptable. Often, what my heart was feeling was not manifested to the world.

A Firm Foundation

Do you carry unwanted baggage concerning your childhood, feeling some level of resentment that brings you pain toward your parents? Everyone has their own perception. I once heard there are three perceptions: yours, theirs, and what is really happening! Each of us perceives the happenings in our own way, depending on our frame of reference. As children, we viewed our parents through a child's eye. As we grew up and developed our own lives, our perceptions changed. Many folks hide their pain, misperceptions, or the entity that is causing them so much grief and heartache. Using our very carefully instilled self-preservation techniques, we may develop some type of addiction. These addictions may develop when our mechanisms kick in to keep us functioning as normally as possible. We need to anesthetize the pain we are experiencing, which is often unbearable. We may try to keep these issues a secret and feel defensive about our family members when we know deep down that our loved ones have serious issues.

Statistics have proven that each member of your household will have a different perception. Being raised in the household will not guarantee we view it in the same light. When I grew into young womanhood, I realized up until then that I had seen the world through my mother's eyes. Having a victim mentality, life was troublesome for her. Our personalities were very different, and much resentment toward me became obvious. I then concluded that, as parents, we do the very best we know how. For me, it was an eye-opening experience that began to set me free.

It is alright to embrace our differences. Each of us develops our own set of boundaries or acceptable behaviors. What is normal to you may not be seen as normal by others. There are universal similarities such as gender, hair color, and educational level, but each family has its own acceptable rules. My family enjoyed hugging and always said "I love you" when coming and going. Many families are not open with their displays of affection. No matter what was going on in my very dysfunctional home, I could count on a hug or an *I love you!* Amidst the very dysfunctional family that I had, I honestly perceived them as normal. It wasn't until I got married and had a home of my own that I realized how totally dysfunctional a family I had grown up in.

Having been raised in church and a pseudo-Christian environment, it was normal for us to stay home on Saturday nights for our baths and to set out our church clothes. We went to church almost every time the doors were open. At least we did get a firm foundation, and for that, I am extremely grateful. Having heard about Jesus from the time I was an infant is the reason I am still serving Christ today. My parents were very concerned about making a good impression, and it became normal to pretend life was wonderful! Embracing our differences was very hard for our family. I needed to understand how my siblings and I could be raised in the same home, but have such different perceptions. I was amazed at how many household chores I performed exactly as my mother did. Then there are many differences in our tastes in interior design.

I have tried to sift out the painful and hurtful memories still imprinted in my mind fifty years later. The fact that we were all created in the image of God does not give us an excuse to intentionally abandon the teachings of our Lord and parents. Because each of us carries different perceptions, it makes it difficult to understand why there are conflicting versions among siblings. The most important fact is that all of us witnessed the power of Christ, which is not perceived any other way other than as the best thing anyone could ever want or need from their raising!

> *Therefore whoever hears these sayings of Mine, and does them, I will liken him to a wise man who built his house on the rock: and the rain descended, the floods came, and the winds blew and beat on that house; and it did not fall, for it was founded on the rock. (Matthew 7:24–25)*

Lord, give me the wisdom to view my parents as human beings, doing the very best they knew how to deal with the issues of raising their children. I am thankful that I was given a firm foundation that has carried me through many trials and tribulations.

Day 31

God Is My Safe Place

Do you realize that everyone deals with insecurity at some point in their life? Many of us have not identified the areas of our insecurities, and some never will. Facing our insecurities can be very painful and heart-wrenching! Just recently, I finally understood my insecurities; it made me feel simply horrible. Looking back on many of my actions that manifested out of my issue stupor, it hit me square between the eyes! I am terribly humiliated now that I think about it. Did people see through me when I acted so inappropriately? The reason that motivated my insecurities was that I always thought that I had to be in the middle of everything. Actually, it was sticking my nose into things that did not concern me and trying to soothe them. More than likely, it was transparent when I thought I hid it very well. Well, truthfully, I did not identify this issue until recently.

For those folks who were violated by my insecurities, they will receive an apology where appropriate. Now that I have identified it, it's time to confront it. Doing a self-inventory and recognizing the signs and feelings associated with my deeply rooted insecurities are now possible. I must put up a stop sign to avoid acting solely out of my severe insecurity. Once I discovered it, I did more than expected and more than required.

People really don't need as much warm fuzzies as I give. So for me, it is time to change those draining emotions that I have acted on one too many times! After putting my plan into action to make the necessary changes, I began to know when they were rising against me. At first, it was difficult to halt what had seemed normal to me for a very long time. It took several times to gain the willpower to stop!

I am freer and feel so much better that I never intend to go back to those old behaviors. Can anyone relate here? Of course you can, because all of us have hidden our insecurities at one time or another. Who do we trust with these bothersome feelings? Well, I hope you already know the answer to that question—Jesus Christ, of course. He is our counselor, our refuge, our confidant, and certainly our very best friend! Why do we feel that, without exhibiting these stupor behaviors, we will be left out? Why do we sometimes feel as if we don't measure up to the standards or unfair expectations placed on us by others?

I decided I was only going to measure up to the standards and principles given to us in the Word of God. Pleasing our Heavenly Father is all that truly matters in this life. People are just too fickle to worry about their expectations. God knows our very core, and more importantly, he understands it completely. The more I strive to be closer to my Lord, the less I feel any pressure to measure up to the opinions of people who are not really important enough to bother with anyway. That's not to say people aren't important, because that would be a false statement. However, when pleasing the Lord, these areas will fall into place. I do care about what my loved ones need or expect of me, but placing totally unrealistic expectations on me and then attempting to put me down because I cannot measure up to their opinions is what I am talking about. At my age, I have learned to conserve my emotional energies for the most important people in my life. First and foremost, living to please my Lord requires my full attention without distractions.

*I will say of the LORD, "He is
my refuge and my fortress, my God,
in whom I trust." (Psalm 91:2)*

Thank you, Lord, for Your clarification on what You expect or desire from us. There is no hidden agenda or ulterior motive behind Your words.

Missing the mark will only separate us from You. I know that You are a God of forgiveness and a God of second chances and more if needed.

* 9 7 9 8 8 9 0 6 1 0 4 6 1 *